I would like to dedicate this book to the many wonderful people who believe in me and who have helped along the way.
With a special thanks to Emma Walker, a very generous friend, who made this possible and my mother for her encouragement and support.

I hope this is the start of many other books. It's been a pleasure creating it for you all to enjoy.

Many thanks,

Leon Prager

Prager's Poetry

By Leon Prager

PRAGER'S POETRY

Contents

A Snail's Tail
The Dog
The Badger
The Fox
The Frog
The Owl
The Sheep
The Flamingo
The Hippo
The Sloth

The Duck
The Rabbit
The Chameleon
The Chicken
The Lion
The Possum
The Armadillo
The Orangutan
The Elephant
The Penguin

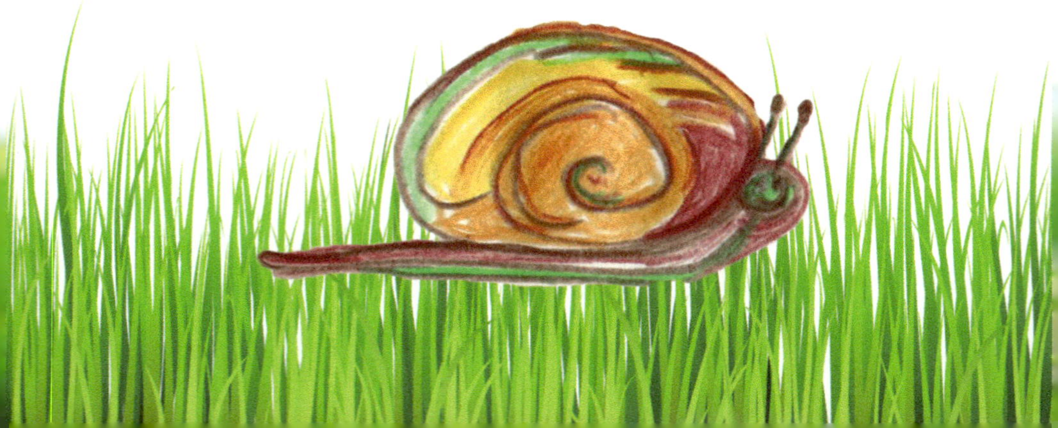

A Snail's Tail

A snail's day is long and slow,
whichever way it may choose to go.
Down the path or through the bush,
this little creature will never rush.

It might be slimy and not very fast,
but its little shell will always last,
so remember it when you walk around,
and for its children's sake, please look down.

The Dog

My dog barks. My dog bites.
My dog doesn't like bright lights.
He can't even defend the porch.
The poor little thing is afraid of a torch.
The little pup poops all over the place.
He wakes me up by licking my face.
He's ace. He's fluffy. He's my best mate.
He's loyal. He's funny. My dog is great.
He's cheeky and quick and steals food from your plate.
He's scary and loud until you open the gate.
We're very alike – in fact, we're the same.
The only difference is I'm wild and he's tame.

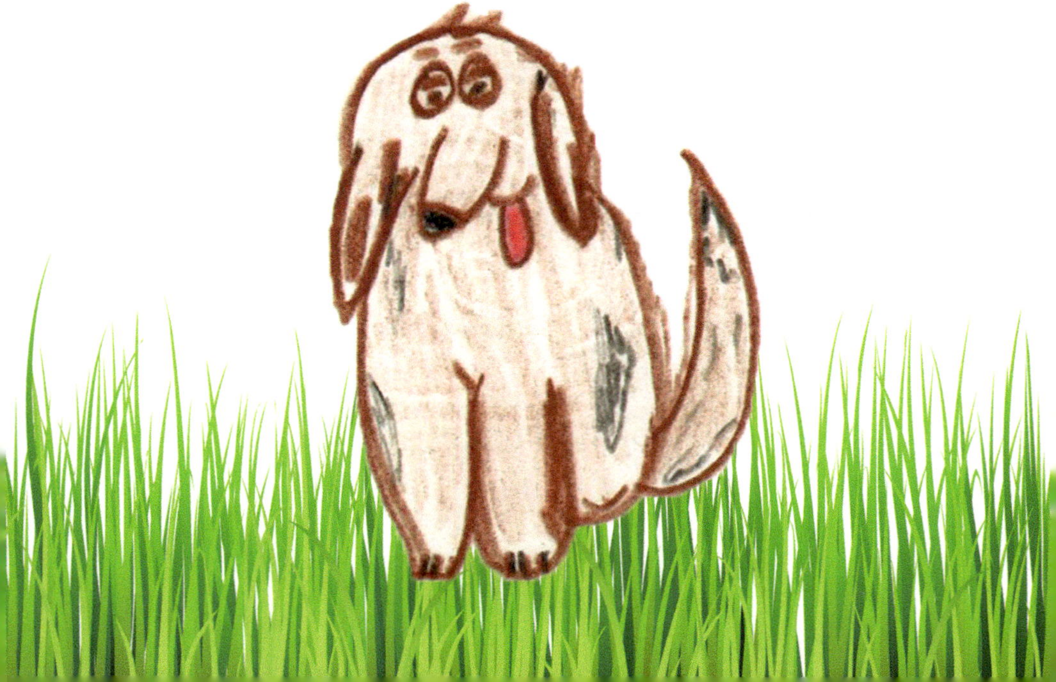

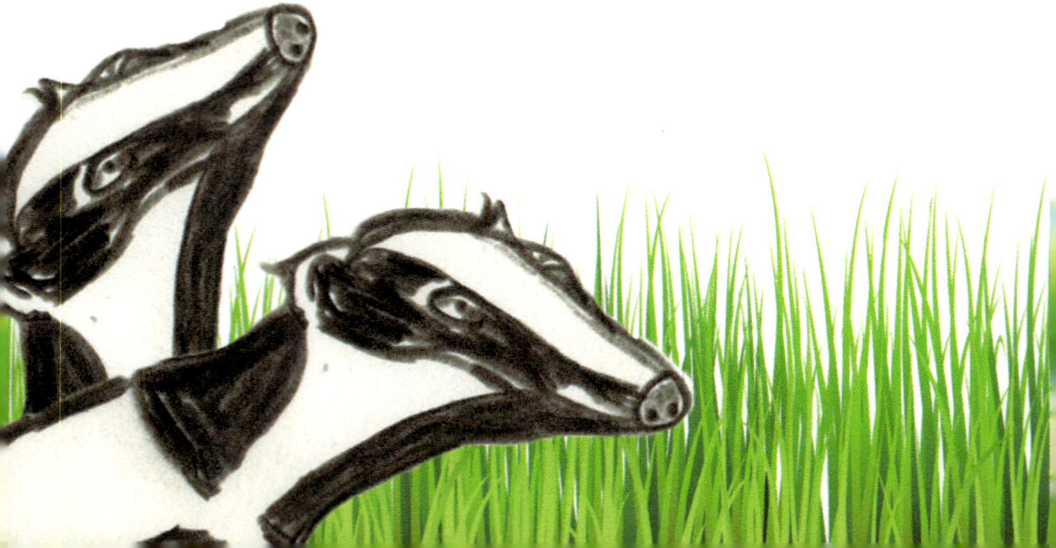

The Badgers

The badgers hide in their holes.
Some of them can climb poles.
Others just like to bite,
and most of them hunt at night.
All of them are pretty shy,
but none of them ever cry
because they know life is rough.
Eating slugs is pretty tough –
or whatever they might have found.
They fight for space underground.
Digging here and digging there,
they always have muddy hair.
They're pretty fierce face-to-face,
so don't get on a badger's case.

The Fox

The fox is sly. The fox is quick.
Don't ask him why.
He's oh-so-slick.
He'll creep from here.
He'll creep from there.
He'll creep off with you unaware.

He might be small. She might be nimble,
full of fight and far from simple.
So next time you meet a fox,
greet it as a big brain box.

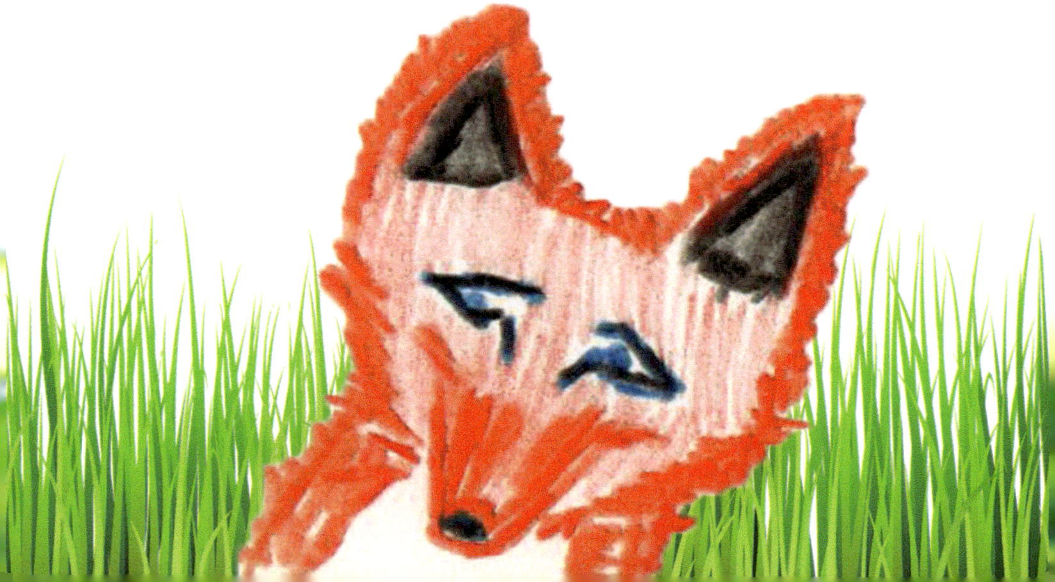

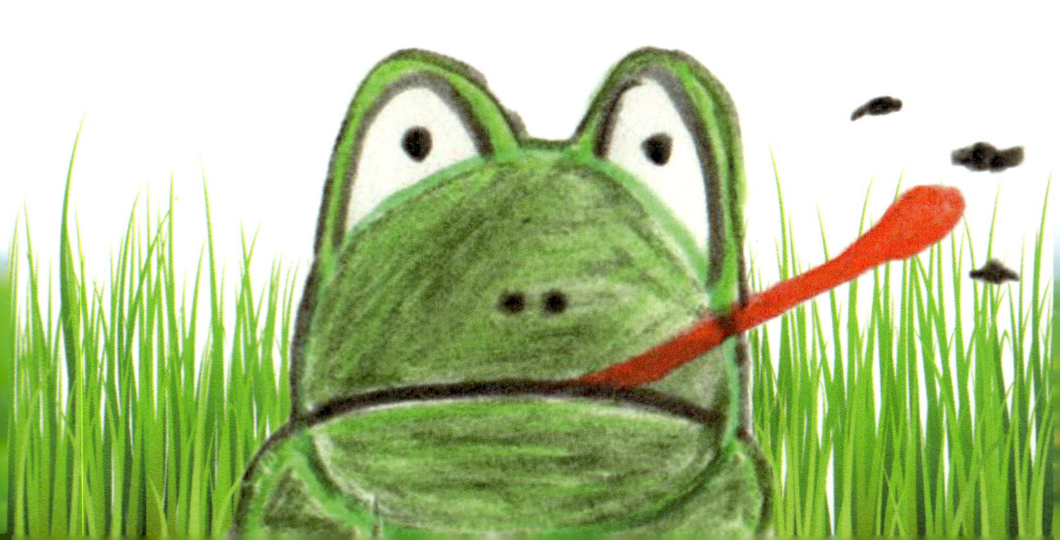

The Frog

I am a little bouncy frog
that lives upon a mouldy log
placed inside a stinking bog
that's shrouded in a cloud of smog,
bouncing from pad to pad.
I never met my mum and dad,
but I'm really not all that sad.
It's all I've ever known and had
since I was a little tad.
I avoid the birds, the fish, the crab.
I'm so quick, it makes them mad.
Come take a dip in my pond,
and we can see the great beyond.

The Owl

The owl is old.
The owl is wise.
The owl can tell when you're telling lies.
So don't be snide and try to hide
behind those eyes that always lie.
The owl sits and waits to catch a mouse
and hesitates above the house
because it knows the mouse will run.
As it goes, the owl knows the outcome –
and yet, it could end in a miss.
But success is full of bliss.
So before you profess to know it all,
remember that you too can fall.
Think twice before you take the risk,
because you may just lose all of this
quicker than a single blink –
so do the work and don't just wish.

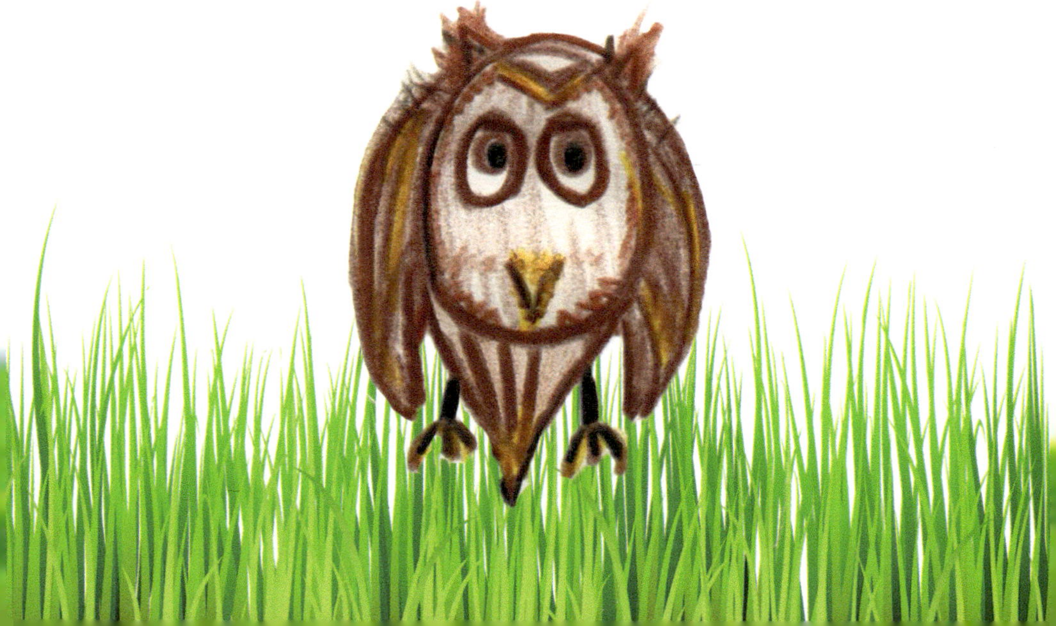

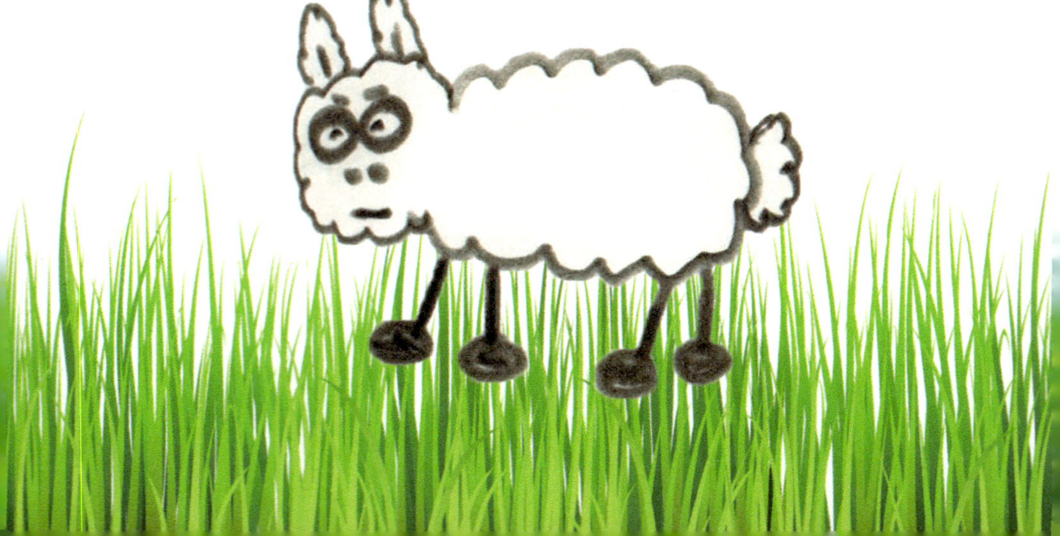

The Sheep

The sheep is fluffy. The sheep is slow.
The sheep has wool which we like to grow.
We take this wool to make our clothes.
Otherwise, most of us would have froze .
We round them up. We pen them in.
We shave them bald. They just can't win.
If things were different, what would they do?
Would we be safe? I've just no clue.

I think they're peaceful. How about you?
I've got some ideas, but just a few.
One wolf could be amongst just two
but hide amongst the larger crew .
If they get scared, they might retreat
back to the land of nod under the sheets.
Here, you can always count on sheep
to help you try and get some sleep.

The Flamingo

I'm a flamingo if you don't know.
I usually stand on just one toe.
My food goes in upside down.
I make a strange laughing sound.
The krill I eat turns me pink,
or so the scientists seem to think.
We flock together in large groups
and get stuck in the mud like pairs of boots.
We like to nibble at grass roots
and fly away when hunters shoot.
We've got no teeth – now, that's the truth.
Between us all, there's not one tooth.
We fly over a thousand roofs in our pursuit to find more food
(to keep us in a happy mood), together in a massive brood.
So keep your distance and don't intrude,
or we might start to think you're rude.
And if you see a flamingo dude,
just know that we all approve
as long as he's not removed,
plucked and cooked, then consumed
by being chewed – the only thing that we can't do.

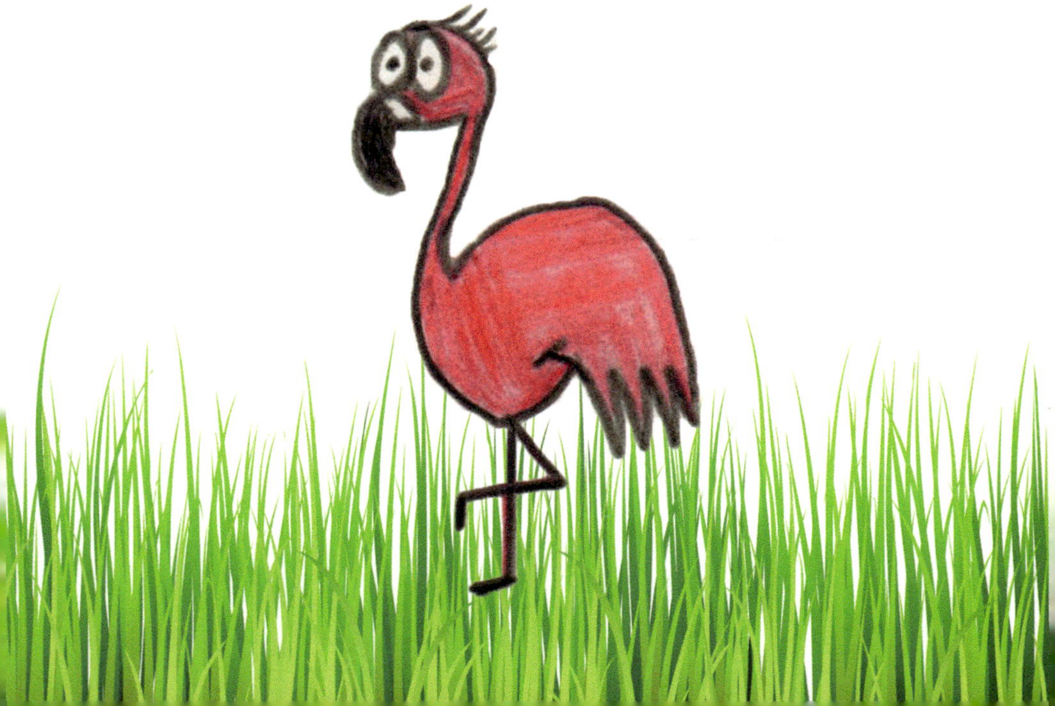

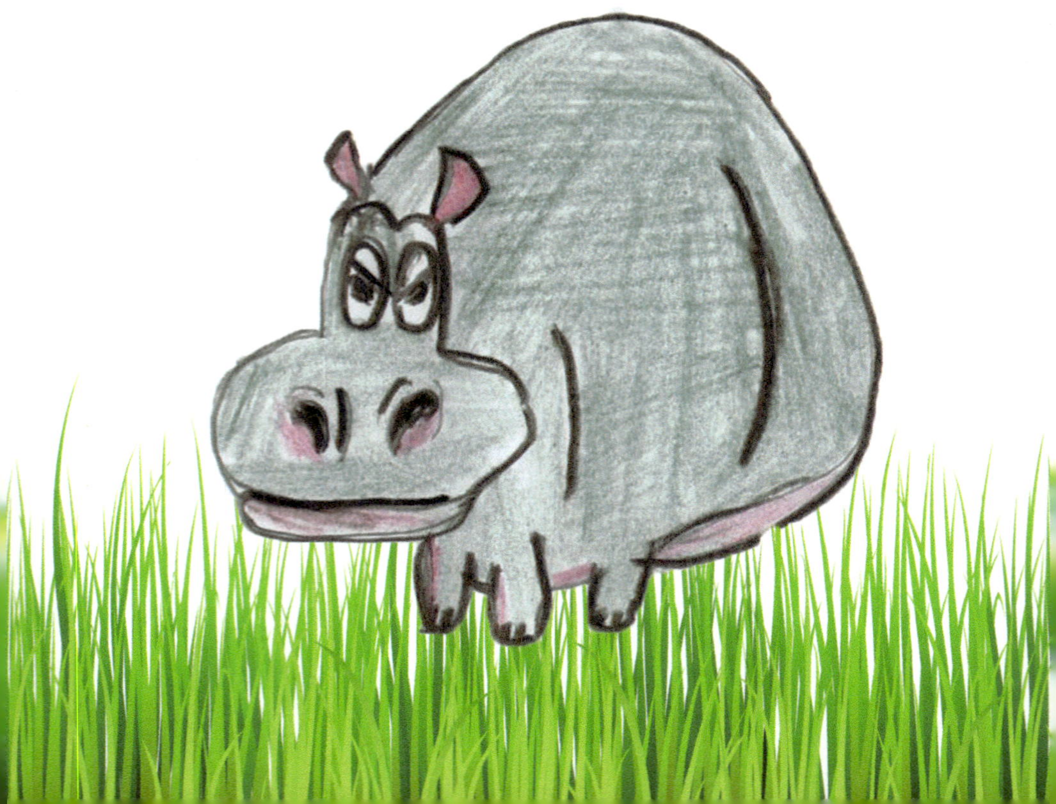

The Hippo

The hippo is heavy. The hippo is large.
The hippo is ready to grunt and then barge.
She's angry at things. She's mean and quite blunt.
Don't get in her way. She's a bit of a runt.

She'll smash you once – probably twice.
I don't like those hippos. They're not very nice.
Protecting their kids, that's all very well,
but would I go back to visit?
There's no chance in hell.

The Sloth

The sloth is lazy. The sloth is slow.
The sloth has fur where algae grow.
It crawls across the trail
at the speed of a snail
with every animal hot on its tail.
It has big claws to hang from trees,
and people like to point at these.
If it was mean and slightly fast,
you might just have to dash.
There's a chance you could get slashed
if it was in an angry stance
or simply hanging from a branch,
the master of the slow dance
and muncher of the local plants.
You can see sloths alone
or collected in buckets.
They're as cute as can be
is the best way to put it.
I'm still in search of my very own puppet,
and if there's a tree, then sloths are sure to be up it.

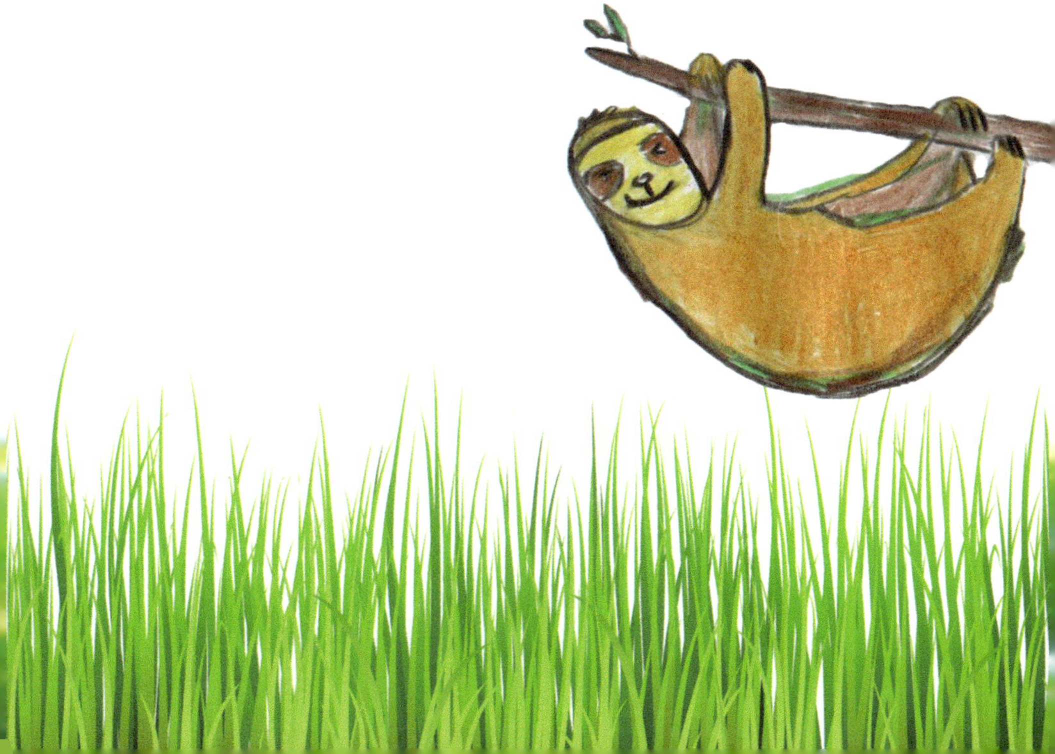

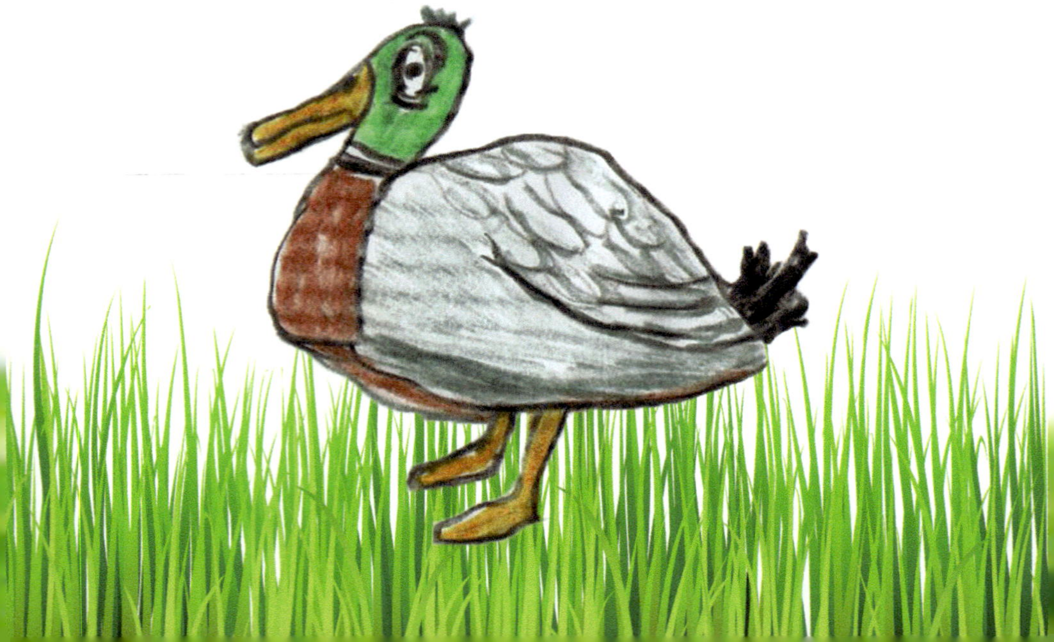

The Duck

Ducks are fluffy from the day that they're born.
They're weatherproofed and designed for a storm.
Their feathers are hollow to help them all float,
and the bread that they swallow just isn't a joke.
They follow their mother's wake with each stroke
and hope to not get lost, get eaten or croak.
You'll see them most days if you live on a boat
or in a big castle that comes with a moat.
They're pretty tough critters when you cook them too long.
I've seen them as slippers and on ponds where they've gone.
I know it's wrong to have them. I can't really lie,
but to eat them is heaven because the meat's never dry.

The Rabbits

Rabbits have habits not unlike our own.
They live in large groups. It's rare they're alone.
They share warmth together in burrows below.
They're as fast as bullets – you can't call them slow.
They help themselves to the veg that we grow,
and people say it's lucky to hold on to a toe.
So if you know a bunny that's funny and cute,
make sure it's not the poor thing that you shoot.
They live under roots in warrens so wide.
They seem to know just how to thrive.
I still hope we decide to be on their side.
Now, let's pray to god that they don't learn to drive.

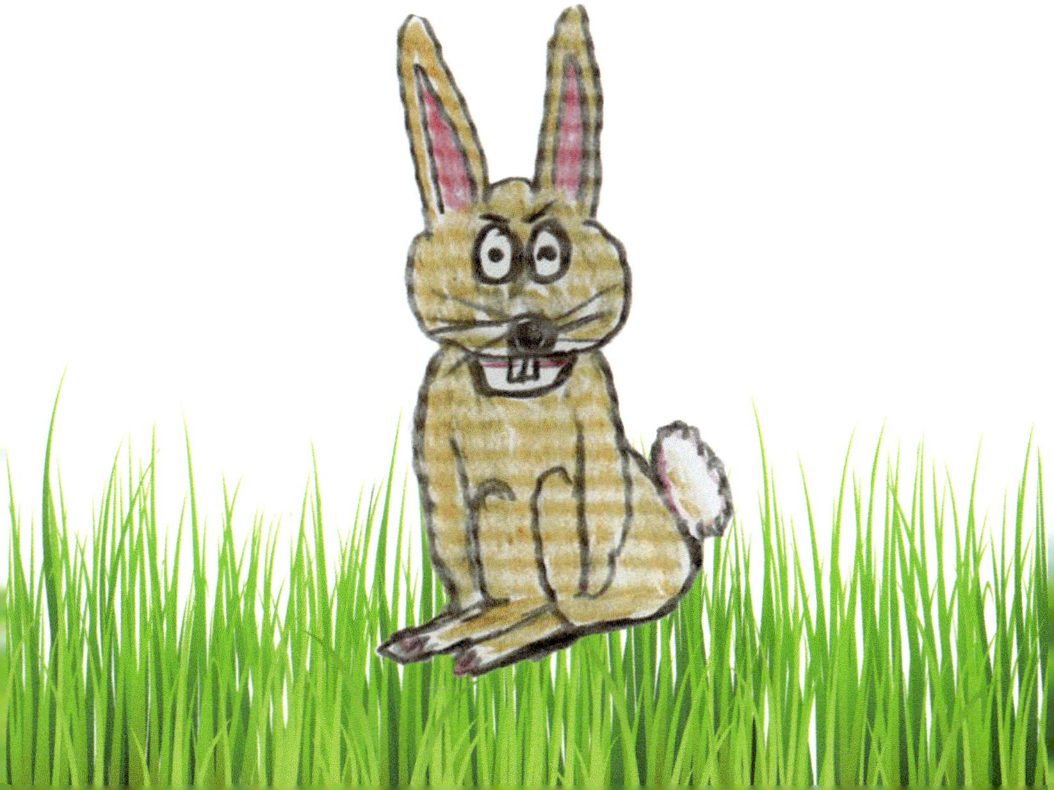

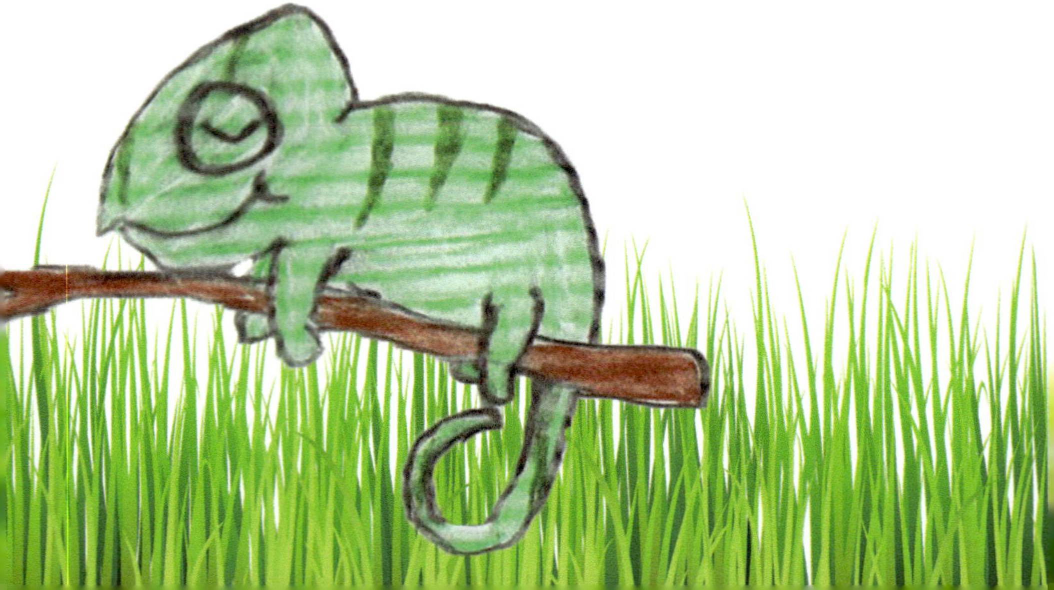

The Chameleon

I'm that smart lizard that knows how to blend.
I can choose many colours, whatever's the trend.
My feet grip the branch like a cute little vice.
I could be your favourite pet for the right kind of price.
My eyes can look all the way round.
There's not a bug in the place that wouldn't be found.
When it's hit by my tongue, then it's sure to go down.
I can pick up on the smallest of sounds.
I look at two things, both at the same time.
One's at the front while the other's behind.
It keeps me safe, well out of harm's way.
Without all these skills, I'd be such easy prey,
but I'm not being killed – well, at least not today.
I'm the camouflage king. I'd be deadly and stealthy,
but there's only one thing:
they gave me a stupid tail instead of a sting.
I can make myself look pale, but I'm still strong and
healthy. You can buy me today, but you'd better be wealthy.

The Chicken

The chicken pecks, thinking "What the heck?"
at breakneck speed. It breaks its neck
to get the seed until it's gone –
a million chickens, not just one.
They try to flap and almost fly,
to pass the gap and not to die,
but soon their fate will be sealed.
It's much too late to change the deal.
So if you like chicken on the bone,
remember this: you're not alone.

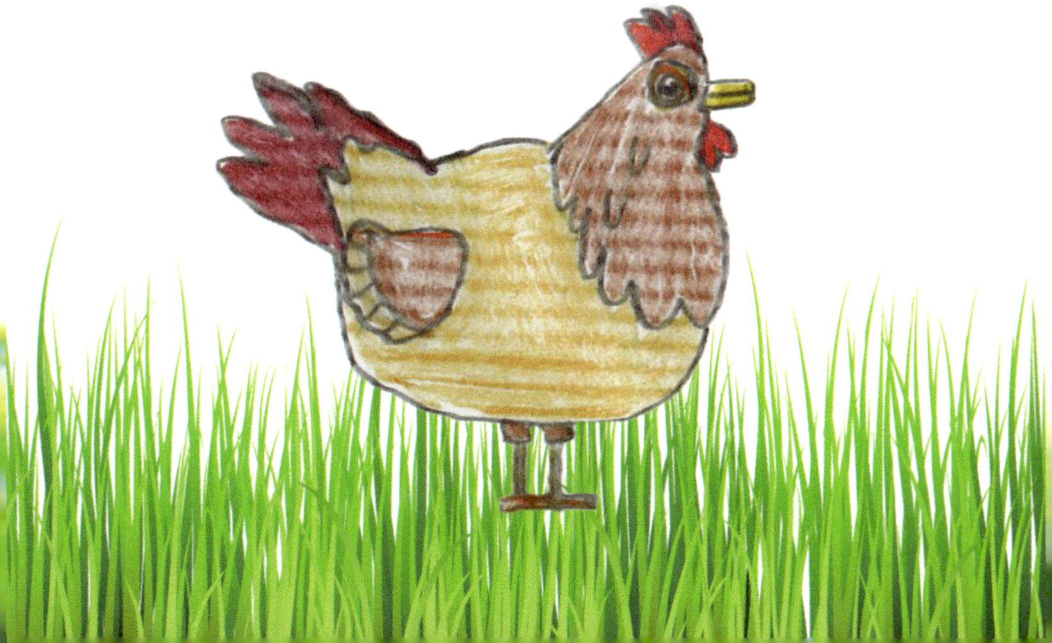

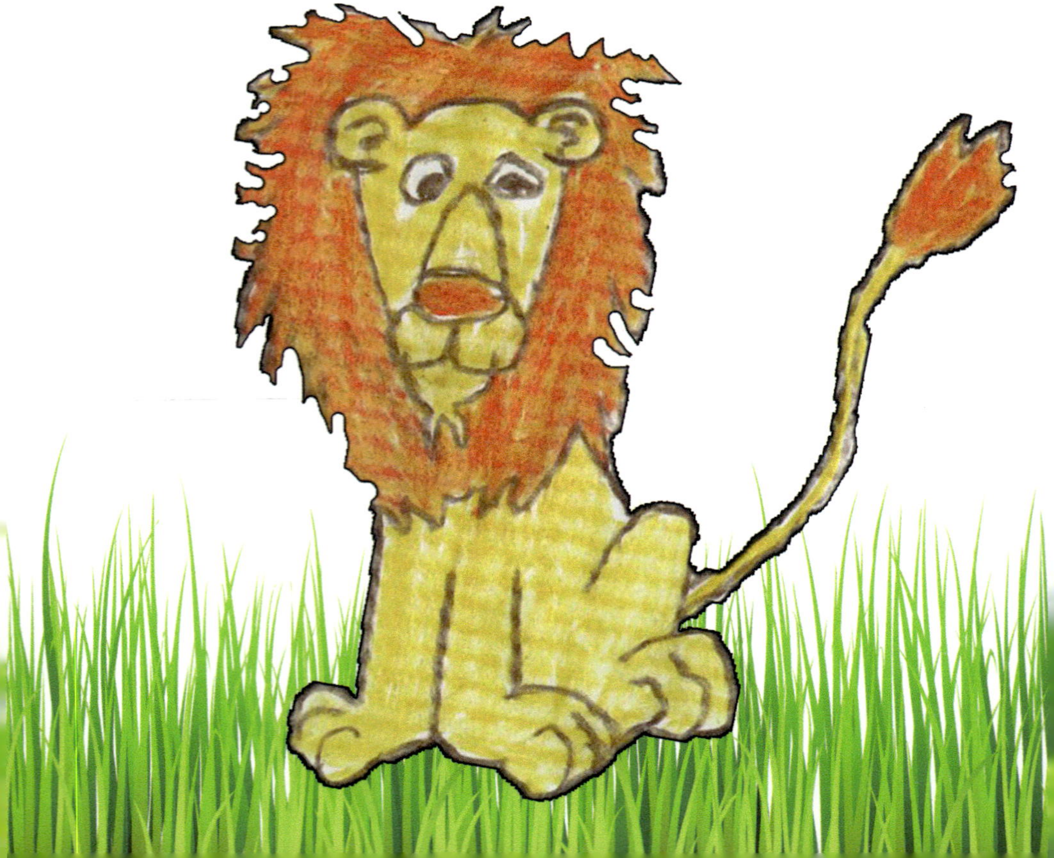

The Lion

The lion's proud to be part of his pride
and lets out a loud roar from deep inside
to show he's alive. He stalks his prey in the night
and sleeps in the day after having a bite.
He lies in the shade and loves a good fight.
The way he behaves just isn't polite.
He strives to survive with all of his might.
It's been tested and tried – this animal's bright,
so to hunt him for a hide just doesn't feel right.
Now put down your gun and please step aside.

The Possum

I saw a possum up in a tree.
The cute little thing was looking at me.
He held very still for more than a while,
then jumped to the fence
with grace and such style.
His sweet little face was sporting a smile.
Quickly, he was gone – just like that, in a flash,
then on the garage.
The possum was back in a dash.
He leaped off into the dark
and joined the other possums
that live in the park.

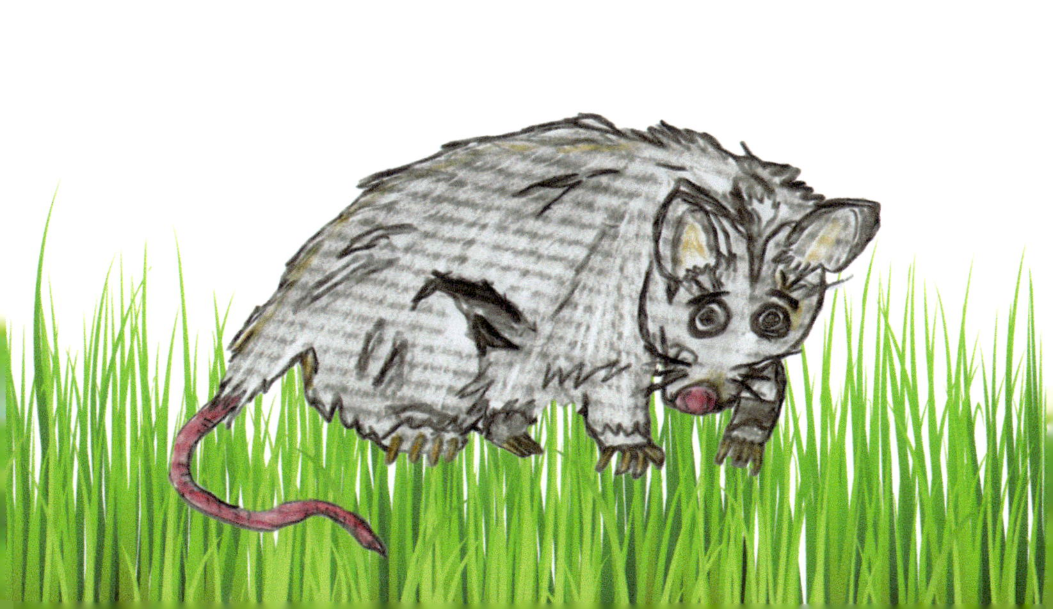

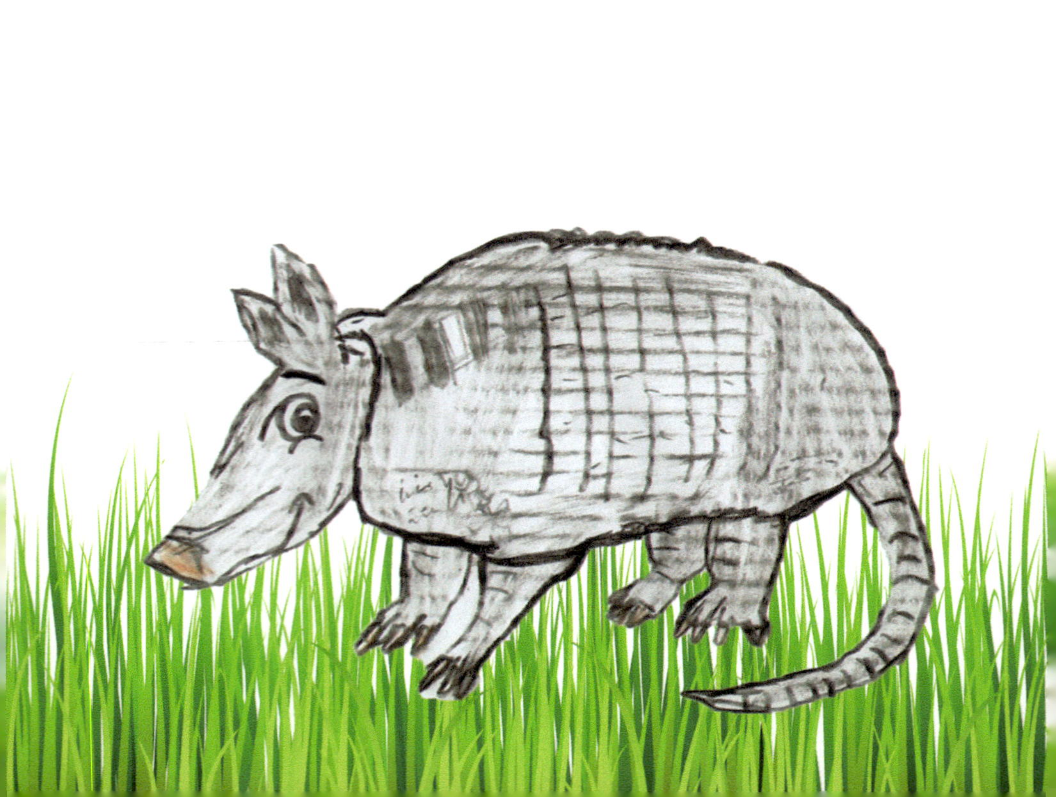

The Armadillo

I'm an armadillo if you can't tell.
I'm covered in an armoured shell.
I'm tough and I roll into a ball
just in case I should fall.
My tongue is long to eat those ants
and maybe some tasty plants.
I live in holes in the ground.
There aren't many of us around.
So if you hear a scurrying sound,
don't worry, it's just an armadillo
somewhere nearby
who is waiting to be found.

The Orangutan

In the trees is where I hang.
I'm a fluffy orange orangutan
swinging from branch to branch.
The other apes don't stand a chance.
I move with grace and never fail.
I don't even have a tail.
A big brain is on the trail.
I entertain on a whole other scale.
I'm in the zoo. I'm in some flicks.
I'm here for you. Come take some pics.
I can even juggle bricks.
I live in a house that is made of sticks.
Just call me Tang – well, that's for short.
It's just the slang for our sort.

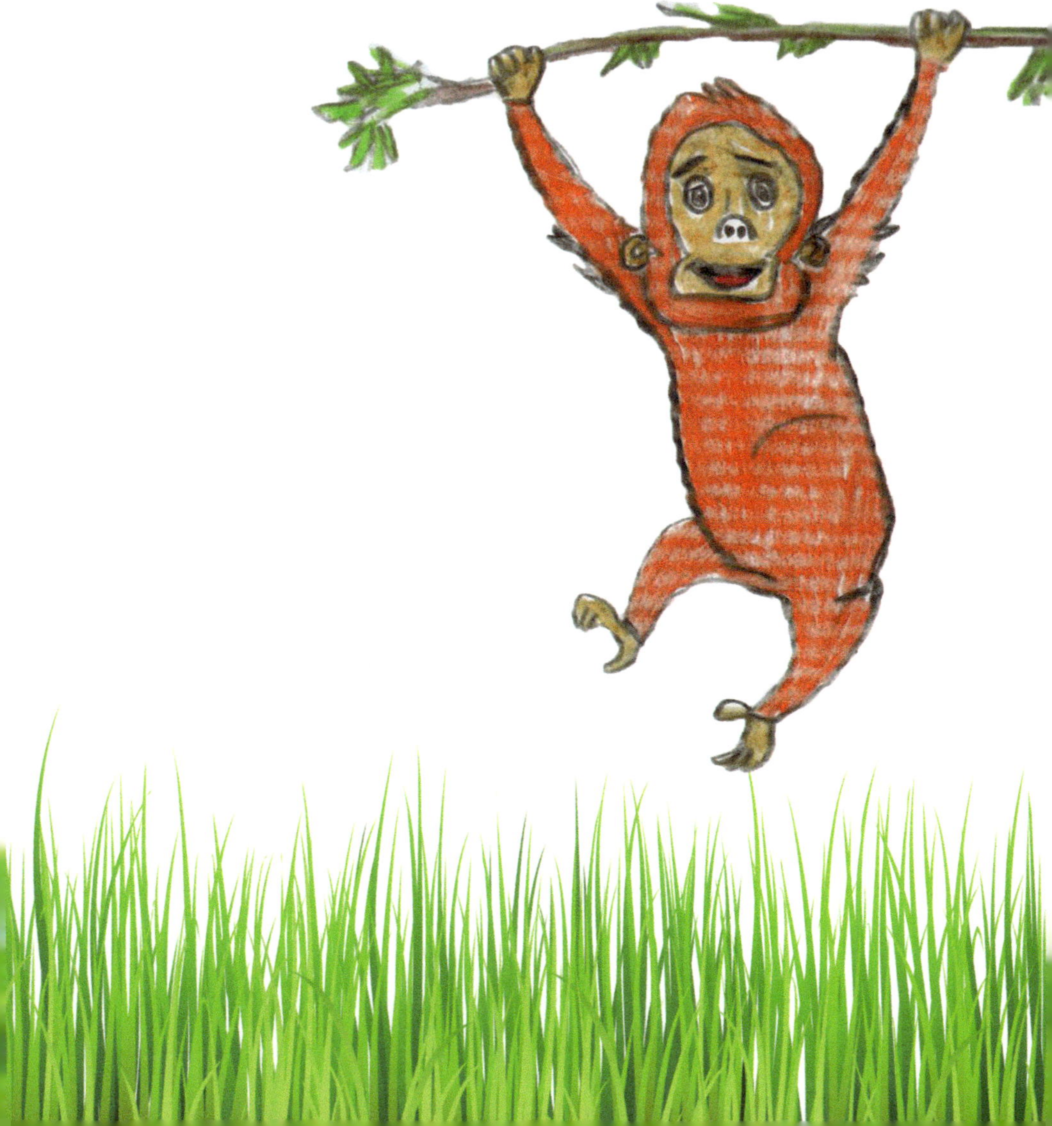

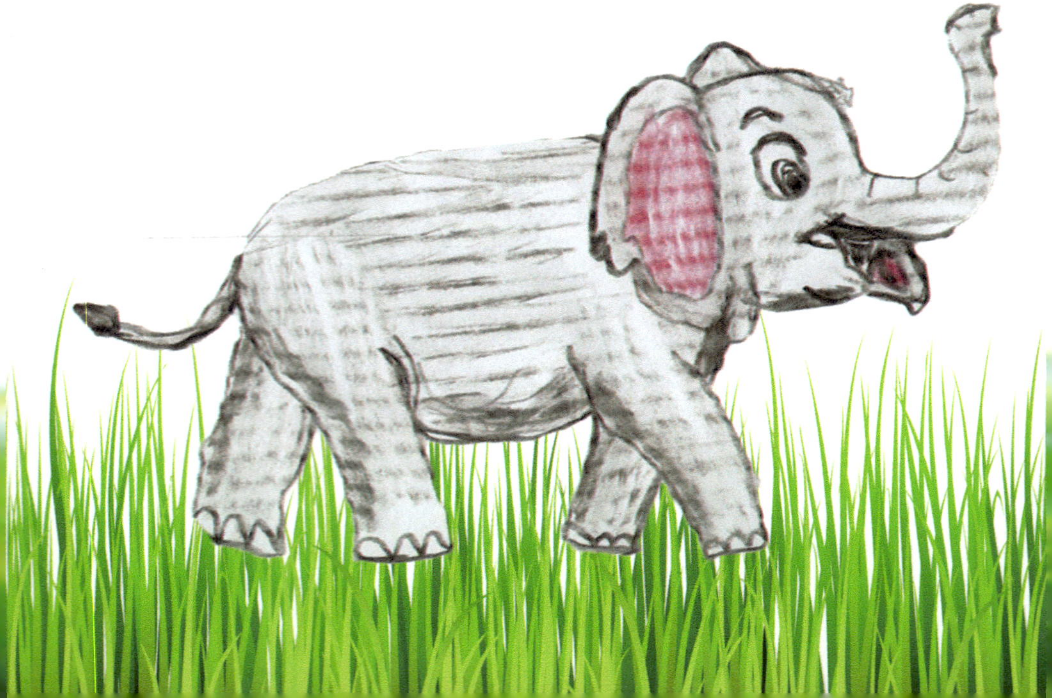

The Elephant

This animal is wide and grey.
It weighs so much and is so tall,
it could knock over a wall.
It mourns for its dead after they're gone
and never forgets where it came from.
It's strong. It's fast. Its life is quite long.
Memories of the past tell it where it belongs.
It loves a good soak but not in the tub.
The soap that it uses is just made of mud.
This creature is the biggest on land,
but still, it follows the command of a man.
I'm just not sure it's part of the plan.
It's never alone – elephants roam in a gang
and knock down the trees
where the monkeys all hang.

The Penguin

The penguin slips.
The penguin slides.
Penguins have so many rides.
Penguins live where it is cold,
young and old and very bold –
or so the stories go. That's what I'm told.
They stand in huddles a thousand strong.
Who knew cuddles could last so long?
So if you're lonely and need a friend,
a penguin is perfect. Let's not pretend.